Tundra Dog

Steve K. Bertrand & Jessie A. Hettinga

Illustrator: Salvador Capuyan

To order additional copies of this book, contact:
Xlibris
844-714-8691
www.Xlibris.com
Orders@Xlibris.com

ISBN: Softcover   978-1-6698-0089-7
         EBook   978-1-6698-0088-0

Print information available on the last page

Rev. date: 03/04/2022

"Saving one dog will not change the world, but surely for that one dog, the world will change forever."

For the Rescuers

It wasn't an easy beginning. She was born in Rankin Inlet, an Eskimo hamlet, on Kudlulik Peninsula, in Nunavut, the most northerly territory in Canada. It was April 1st, 2018, also known as "April Fools' Day". But there was no fooling about this day. At least not if you were talking about the weather. It was very, very cold in this subarctic climate. In fact, on the day the little dog was born, it was just five degrees Fahrenheit.

Native Eskimos referred to Nunavut as "Our Land", & had lived here for 4,000 years. These "Paleo-Eskimos" had migrated with their spears, bows & dogs from Asia during the Ice Age, across the Bering Strait, through Alaska, & down to this treeless region, this tundra of land, ice & water, known as Nunavut.

The people made a living hunting, fishing & mining. It was a harsh land, the land of the white whale, grizzly bear & bald eagle. The little dog was born to a litter of five pups, a Chihuahua & Rat Terrier mix, under the porch of the Hudson General Store. Right from the beginning, she had to fend for herself. One by one, the other pups had wandered off. Their mother had not returned one evening from daily hunting.

The little dog had been living off rodents she could catch, table scraps tossed into yards by villagers, & the generosity of the man who owned the general store. She ate snow, drank from puddled water near buildings, or dripping pipes. At night, when temperatures dropped below zero degrees, she curled up & shivered through the cold & dark beneath the porch of the general store, falling asleep to the sound of mice scurrying around the building.

At dawn, she'd awaken & sometimes wander down to the docks & watch the fishermen as they headed out in their boats for a day of fishing at sea. Other times, she'd follow the miners as they trudged off to the local mines. But what she enjoyed most was trotting up the hillside outside town to the rough stones stacked in the form of a human by the Eskimo people long ago. It was a landmark the Inuits called "Inukshuk", & it signified safety, hope & friendship. The locals referred to it as "The Gateway to the North". For some reason, the little dog felt safe here.

From here, she often sat & gazed down upon the buildings & people that made up the village of Rankin Inlet. From here she could watch the boats come & go from Hudson Bay. Sometimes, beyond the snowdrifts, she gazed upon the Aurora Borealis, or "Northern Lights", as they danced across the sky. Always, she had to be on guard. There were predators. Hawks circled overhead. Wolves roamed the land. Polar bears swam in the sea.

Not everyone was friendly. The local butcher often chased her from his door. What she learned was — how to fend for herself; &, to trust her instincts. What she learned was — how to brace against the cold, hunger & loneliness.

Then, one afternoon, as she was returning from the pile of stones on the hillside, a woman was sitting on the porch of the general store. Her black hair was braided. She wore a heavy parka, & her pants were tucked into boots. When she saw the scrawny, little, black—haired dog, she smiled & held out her hands. The little dog stopped in her tracks. Should she trust this woman? She wasn't exactly a stranger. The woman shopped at the general store. The little dog had seen her come & go carrying sacks of goods. They called her "Ahnah". "Ahnah Crow". She was Eskimo.

Ahnah continued to smile & hold out her hands. Trusting her instincts, the little dog approached the woman. Closer... Closer... Closer... She stopped at Ahnah's muddy boots. Ahnah reached down & softly petted the little dog's head. The little dog stood very still, prepared to bark, bite or run, if necessary. "Aren't you a doll," said Ahnah, as she reached down & picked up the little dog. Ahnah drew her close & cradled the little dog in her arms. The little dog thought she smelled of earth, sea & sky. Ahnah patted her back. "Good doggy," said Ahnah. She reached in her coat pocket, pulled out a piece of beef jerky, & gave it to the dog.

As Ahnah petted her head, the little dog sat in her lap & chewed on the jerky. For the first time in her life, the little dog felt herself begin to relax. It felt good to sit in Ahnah's lap. Safe, warm & comforting. "Yes, you are a real doll," said Ahnah.

Just then, the owner of the general store came out on the porch. "Any idea who owns this pup?" asked Ahnah. "No one," said the store owner. "It's a stray. Lives under my porch. I've been feeding it. Guess it's free for the taking." Ahnah eyed the dog. "Well... with a husband, three dogs & two cats, the last thing I need is another mouth to feed. Still... I think I'll take it home," Ahnah said, scratching the dog's ear. "We'll figure something out. Even if it's only until we can find it a home, at least it's better than living under your porch."

Ahnah got up off the porch with the dog. The little dog continued gnawing on the jerky. As Ahnah began walking away, the man hollered — "Watcha gonna call it?" Ahnah stopped. Looked at the little dog, then, at the man. "Well... It's a girl," Ahnah said. I was thinking I'd call her... 'Dolly'." And with that, the little dog was named. The store owner smiled & nodded. Ahnah turned & headed down the dirt road toward home carrying Dolly. They walked for quite a while.

Finally, they arrived at a small cabin on the outskirts of town. It was located close to the sea. Both the cabin & yard were blanketed with snow. The husband made a living fishing. He was Eskimo too. There were three dogs lying in the snowy, front yard. As Ahnah approached, they got up & trotted up to her. They could see she was holding something. Dolly didn't know what to think. Were they friendly? She burrowed into Ahnah's arms. "Don't worry," said Ahnah. She reached down & patted each dog on the head. She showed them Dolly. "Here's a new playmate," she said. "But, it's only temporary. Only until we can find a home." The dogs sniffed at Dolly. "Be nice," said Ahnah. "Her name is 'Dolly'." Ahnah took Dolly into the cabin. The other dogs followed. They eyed Dolly suspiciously. Even the cats seemed leery. They turned their backs on Dolly & went about their business.

When Ahnah's husband, Richard, came home from fishing, he simply looked at Dolly & said, "Another mutt; another mouth to feed." Like the animals, he didn't pay Dolly much attention. Dolly retreated to a corner of the cabin. Here Ahnah had placed a blanket, water bowl & food dish for Dolly. Dolly did her best to stay out of everyone's way. She didn't feel very welcome. Thank goodness for the friendliness of Ahnah.

True to her word, Ahnah began looking for a home for Dolly. She talked to neighbors. Posted signs in the general store. Made phone calls. However, everyone she talked to already had a cat or dog. Then, one day while Ahnah was in the general store, the owner pointed to a poster on the wall. He knew Ahnah was having trouble finding a home for Dolly. "You might talk to these people," he said. "They're an animal rescue group in Port Coquitlam, just east of Vancouver, British Columbia. They'll find a good home for Dolly."

Ahnah looked at the flyer. The organization was called "The Canine Rescue Project". Sure enough, they were out of Port Coquitlam; but, that was over a thousand miles away. "What could they do?" thought Ahnah. Still, Ahnah wrote down the phone number on the wall & tucked it into her jacket pocket. When she got home that afternoon, she called the number. The man who answered the phone listened as Ahnah talked about Dolly. He took down all her information. Then, he informed Ahnah they wouldn't be able to respond right away. They had quite a list of dogs they were attempting to rescue & place in homes. Ahnah thanked the man & hung up.

However, weeks passed by. Weeks turned into months. The days grew warmer. Spring turned into summer. Summer turned into fall. Fall turned into winter. Still, there was no word from the animal shelter. Then, one afternoon the phone rang. It was the man from The Canine Rescue Project. His name was Arty Graham. He informed Ahnah he would be flying up to Rankin Inlet the following week. Could he pick Dolly up then? Ahnah said, "Yes". When she hung up the phone, a lump formed in her throat. She'd grown quite attached to Dolly. But, a promise was a promise.

Arty Grahm arrived at Rankin Inlet Airport on a very cold February day. In fact, the temperatures were minus eleven degrees Fahrenheit. Ahnah brought Dolly to the airport. It was a very sad moment. However, Ahnah reminded herself — "I've done a good thing saving Dolly. These people will find her a good home." Dolly didn't understand what was happening. She liked Ahnah. She didn't like it when she was handed off to the man by the airplane. Arty boarded the plane with Dolly. He carried her to the back of the plane. Here he placed her in a metal kennel for the trip to Port Coquitlam. Dolly wandered the kennel. She didn't understand why she was separated from Ahnah. She was very afraid. The plane ride was a bit bumpy. However, the plane finally arrived at Vancouver International Airport. From there, Arty drove to Port Coquitlam. Dolly remained in the kennel in the back of the van.

When they arrived at The Canine Rescue Project, Arty carried Dolly into the building. There were quite a few dogs in kennels. Little Dogs. Big Dogs. Shaggy Dogs. Hairless dogs. All eyes were on Dolly as Arty carried the kennel into the room. Once again, Dolly felt those long-ago fears returning. Why had things changed? She paced back & forth in her cage. Arty brought Dolly & the other dogs food & water. He left a light on in the animal shelter; then, went home. Dolly settled down for the night. She went to sleep thinking — "What will tomorrow bring?"

In the morning, a family arrived. They had driven for about an hour to The Canine Rescue Project from Point Roberts, USA. Arty brought the man, woman, two boys & a girl into the shelter. They stood around the cage talking while Dolly stared up at them. Dolly heard her name mentioned several times while they talked, gazing & pointing her direction. Finally, the woman nodded. And, with that, the children began smiling & jumping up & down. Arty reached down & opened the cage. Dolly didn't know what to do. She remained in the cage. That's when the girl reached into the cage & grabbed Dolly. She brought her out of the cage & held her close. The boys gathered around & petted Dolly. Dolly felt the way she did when she was held by Ahnah.

Arty walked the family to the parking lot. Dolly was loaded into a different kennel in the back of their truck. Arty waved good—bye as the family drove away. As they headed home, the children peered over the back seat & talked excitedly to Dolly. Dolly gazed up smiling. She liked these people.

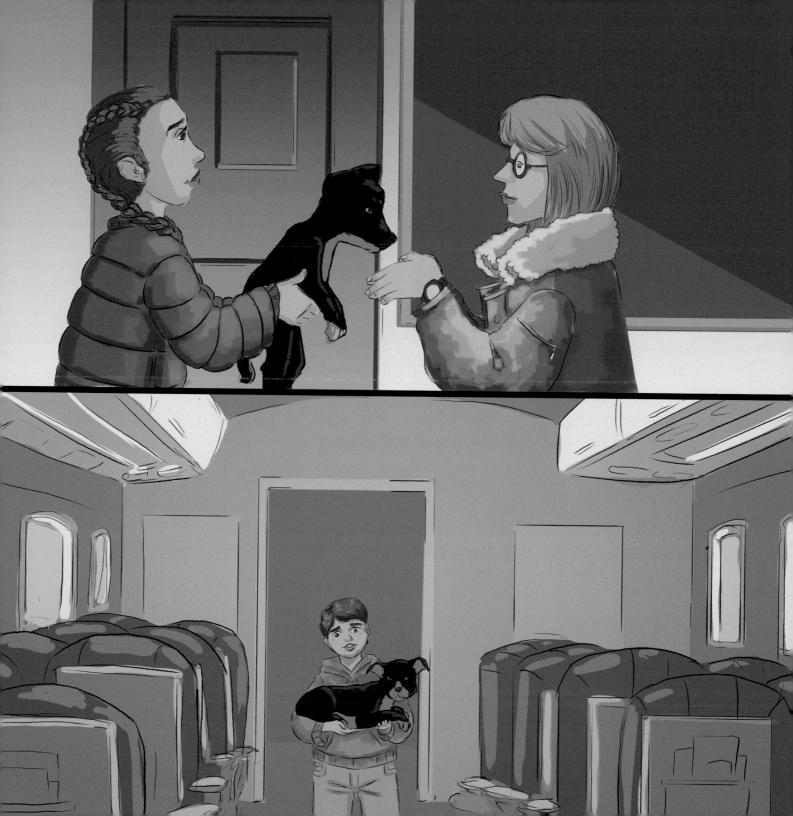

When the family arrived home, they took Dolly out of her kennel. The mother held the dog. The family gathered around Dolly. They were the Brandt family. They were all smiling as they took turns petting Dolly. They lived in a big house. It was brand new. The husband had just finished building it. They also had a huge front yard. In the front yard was a big dog, an English chocolate lab. His name was "Tave". He trotted up to the family. The mother showed Dolly to Tave. Tave smiled. He wagged his tail & gave a friendly bark. In the windowsill sat two cats. They watched the arrival of Dolly. It was hard to tell what they were thinking.

The first thing the Brandt family did was take Dolly to the local veterinary clinic. Here she was bathed, had her toenails clipped, & received her vaccinations. Though Dolly only weighed three pounds upon arrival, the vet gave her a clean bill of health. Dolly felt like a new dog! Her fur had a shiny, black sheen.

When they got home, the Brandt family put Dolly & Tave on leashes & walked them around the neighborhood. Later, they took the dogs down to the beach. It didn't take long for Dolly to feel accepted. She went everywhere with the family. To show her happiness, Dolly often raced around the house chasing the cats & children, as she barked excitedly. She'd ride to the grocery store with the mother, play fetch in the yard with the kids, & wrestle with Tave in the front yard. Even the cats liked her. And, in the evenings, after a day of play & adventure, she sat in the husband's lap in his favorite easy chair, as he scratched her ears till they both fell asleep. Yes, finally, Dolly was home.

Epilogue

A rescue dog is a dog who has been placed in a new home after being neglected, abused or abandoned by a previous owner. There are many animal rescue organizations that care, protect & rescue dogs. Evidence shows that rescue dogs can remember aspects of their past. Adopted dogs are very grateful & loving toward individuals & families who save them. Only 1 out of every 10 dogs will find a permanent home. Approximately 4 million dogs enter animal shelters every year. Of those 4 million, 1.6 million are adopted each year. According to The Humane Society, there are approximately 3,500 animal shelters in the United States; & 10,000 rescue groups & animal sanctuaries in North America.

Printed in the United States
by Baker & Taylor Publisher Services